In a Chinese Alphabet

the first stroke is RED,

the second stroke is YELLOW,

the third stroke is BLUE,

the fourth stroke is GREEN,

the fifth stroke is ORANGE,

the sixth stroke is PURPLE.

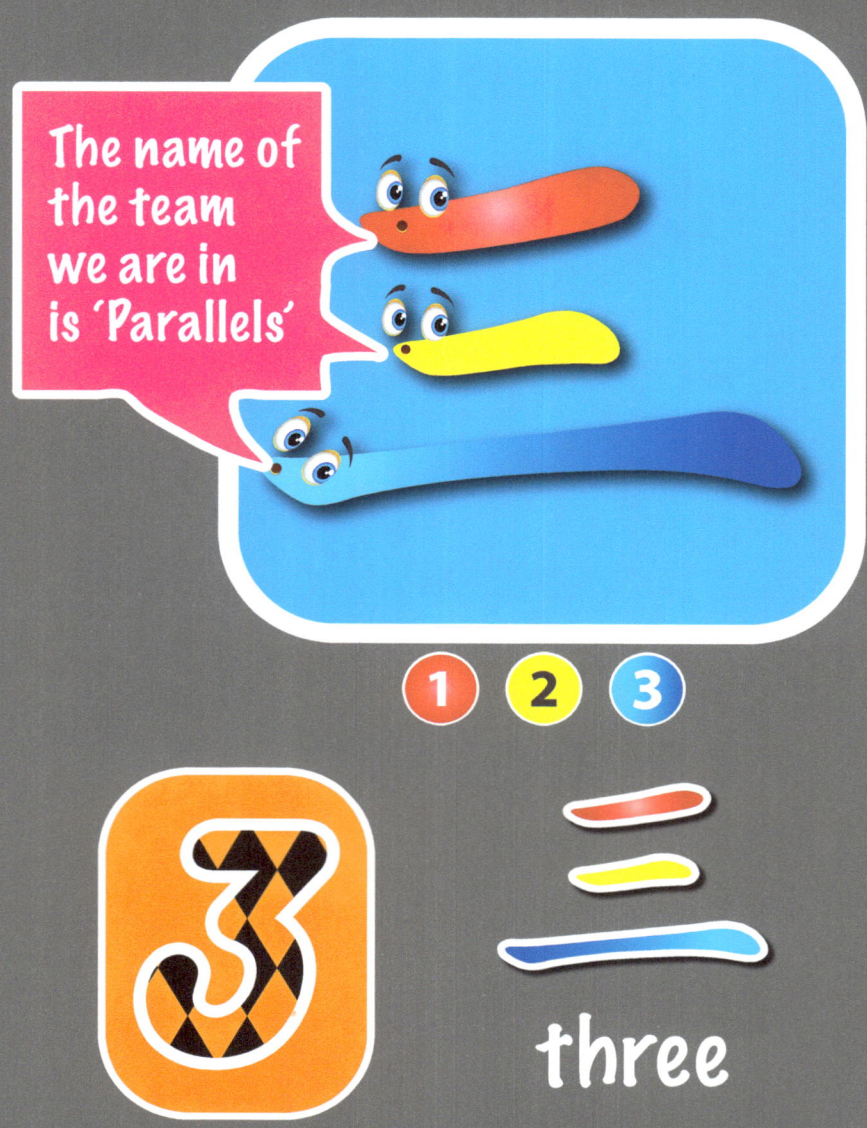

② Dots (Left to Right)

Look out for us in the word below

① ②

6   六

six

3 Dots (Top to Bottom)

① ②

fly

④ Final Dot

cloud

⑤ Half Ladder

6 T-Shape

Look out for us in the Chinese word for 5

five

⑦ Split

> I stretch to the right

> I stretch to the left, we are doing a 'Split'.

eight

⑨ Slide

Do we look like a slide?

① ②

水
water

⑩ Cross

叉
fork

11 7-Slash Split

I'm 7-Slash

Can you see me? I'm hidden here!

① ② ③

many

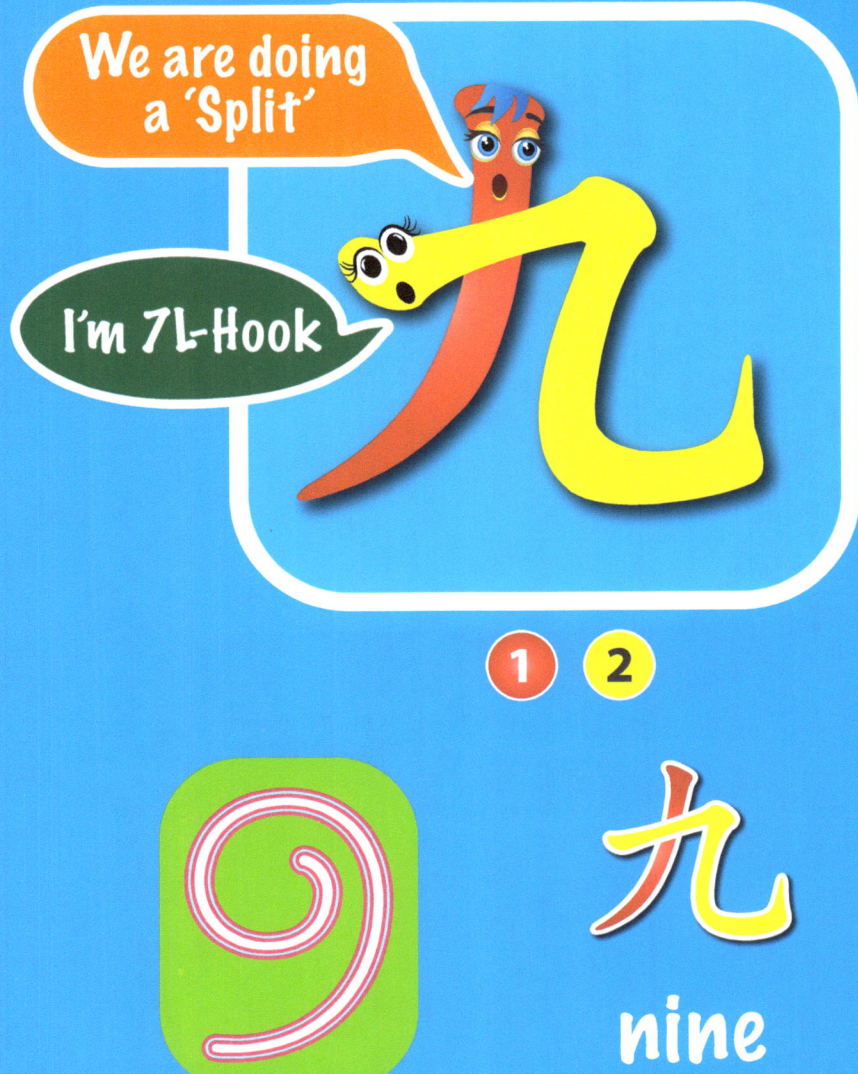

13 Marching

① ② ③

spear

14 Ti**ck**

to sweep

15 7-Hook Flag

I'm 7-Hook ...
I'm the flag ...

I'm the flag pole.

① ②

爷爷

grandfather

⑰ 7-Hook Frame

刀
knife

⑱ U-Frame

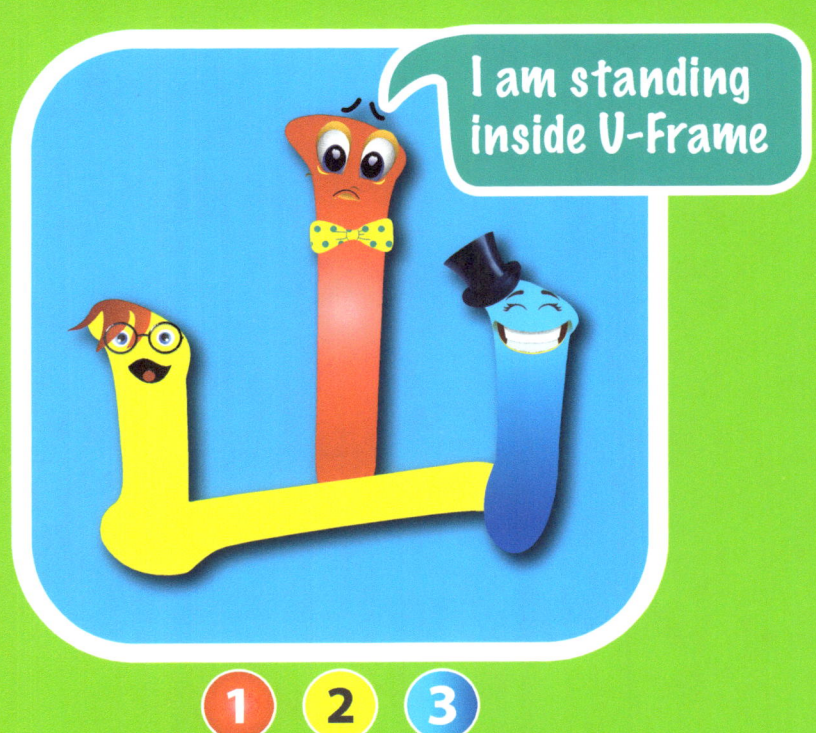

I am standing inside U-Frame

1 2 3

mountain

⑳ Flipped-C

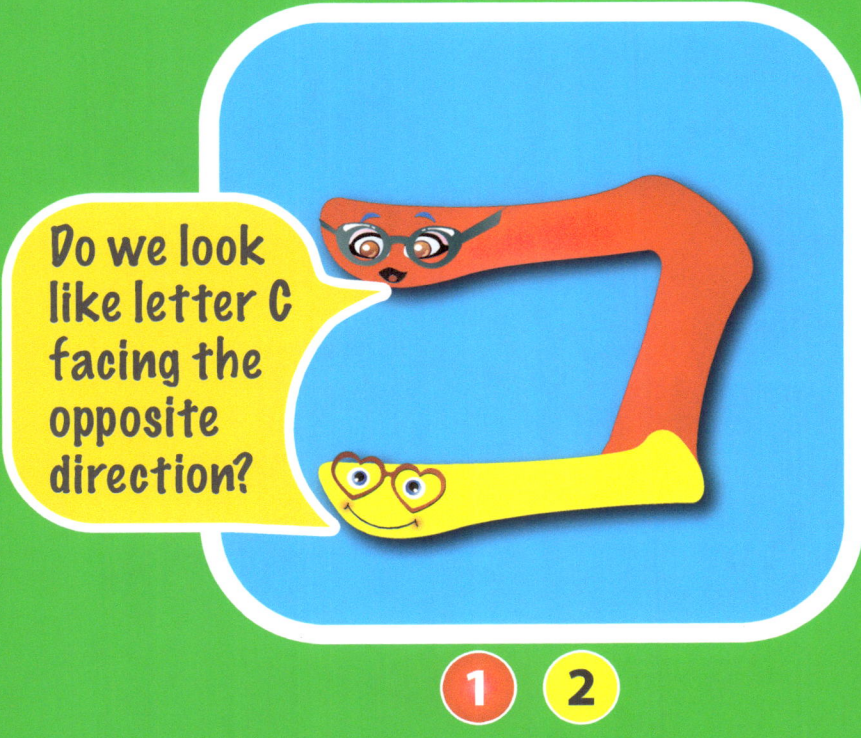

Do we look like letter C facing the opposite direction?

① ②

ruler

21 L7-Hook Frame

I am L7-Hook

① ②

horse

㉒ LZ-Enclosure

I am 7-Hook

I am L-Bend

① ② ③

母牛

COW

23 n-Frame

I support the n-Frame above me

① ② ③

mouth

㉔ Skewer

I stand upright and pierce through others

① ② ③

毛巾
towel

25. Single Leg

Standing on one leg

ten

26 Multiple Legs

Standing on two legs

① ② ③ ④

to open

27 Split Intersections

Intersecting the Split

big

㉙ Flat Intersections

I am flat on the floor. I support everyone above me.

① ② ③

土
earth

30 Horizontals Enclosure

sun

31 Verticals Enclosure

> We are the Verticals inside the enclosure

box

 Intersections Enclosure

We intersect inside the enclosure

① ② ③ ④ ⑤

fish

Remember us?
We are the first Chinese Alphabet you meet in our team Parallels.

Meet the other basic members in our team

Hello!
Find out more about us in the next book!
See you!

① Parallels

www.ingramcontent.com/pod-product-compliance
Lightning Source LLC
Chambersburg PA
CBHW042040050526
44107CB00107B/1040